Music Makers

Helen Maxey

OXFORD
UNIVERSITY PRESS

OXFORD
UNIVERSITY PRESS

Great Clarendon Street, Oxford OX2 6DP

Oxford University Press is a department of the University of Oxford.
It furthers the University's objective of excellence in research,
scholarship, and education by publishing worldwide in

Oxford New York

Auckland Bangkok Buenos Aires Cape Town Chennai
Dar es Salaam Delhi Hong Kong Istanbul Karachi Kolkata
Kuala Lumpur Madrid Melbourne Mexico City Mumbai
Nairobi São Paulo Shanghai Taipei Tokyo Toronto

Oxford is a registered trade mark of Oxford University Press
in the UK and in certain other countries

British Library Cataloguing in Publication Data

Data available

ISBN 0 19 917463 6

10 9 8 7 6 5 4 3 2

Also available in packs
Sports and Leisure Mixed Pack (one of each book) ISBN 0 19 917464 4
Sports and Leisure Class Pack (six of each book) ISBN 0 19 917465 2

www.oup.com/uk/primary

Printed in China

Acknowledgements

The Publisher would like to thank the following for permission to reproduce photographs:
p 3 Pictorial Press; p 4 Marc Romanelli/Getty Images (top), Bruno De Hoques/Getty Images (bottom); p 5 Northern Heritage
by Maureen Corbett (bottom); p 6 Topham/Photonews; p 7 Corbis (top), Odile Noel/Redferns (bottom); p 8 Stefan Diller/AKG
London (left), Museo di San Marco dell'Angelico,Italy/Bridgeman Art Library (right); p 9 Steve Benbow/Photolibrary Wales
(top), Robert Holmes/Corbis (bottom); p 10 Anthony Crickmay/Music Company London Ltd. (top), Erich Lessing/AKG London
(bottom); p 11 Visioars/AKG London (top), AKG London (bottom); p 12 AKG London; p 13 Paul Mellon Collection/Bridgeman
Art Library (top), Erich Lessing/AKG London (bottom); p 14 Fitzwilliam Museum/Bridgeman Art Library; p 15 Reuters/
Popperfoto (top), Sony Picture Classics/ Moviestore Collection (bottom); p 16 Corel; p 17 AKG London (top), Quartet
Solaris/Kate Mount/Lebrecht Music Collection (bottom); p 18 Erich Lessing/AKG London (top), Colette Masson/Euguerand
(bottom); p 19 Erich Lessing/AKG London (top), David Mees/The Cobbe Collection (bottom); p 20 Veronica Jones/Getty
Images (top), The Bridgeman Art Library (bottom); p 21 Mary Evans Picture Library (top), Clive Barda/Performing Arts library
(bottom); p 22 J.G.Fuller/Hutchison Picture Library; p 23 Linda Rich/Performing Arts Library (top), Clive Barda/Performing Arts
Library (bottom); p 24 Odeon/Pictorial Press Ltd (top), Aquarius Library (bottom); p 25 David Redfern/Redferns (top), Corbis
(bottom); p 26 RA/Lebrecht Collection (top), David Redfern/Redferns (bottom); p 27 AKG London (top), Paul Bergen/Redferns
(bottom); p 28 Pictorial Press Ltd (top), John Frost Newspapers Ltd (bottom); p 29 Roberta Parkin/Redferns (bottom)

Front cover photograph of Sophie Colbourne by Neil Turner/TSL Education
Back cover by Erich Lessing/AKG London

Picture research by Debra Weatherley

Contents

Anyone can be a musician! As long as you can make sound, you can make music.

Rhythm and beat

Do you tap your foot in time to music? If so, you are responding naturally to the music's pulse or beat. The beat can be very heavy, as in rock music, or fast, as in some dance music, or slow, as in a funeral march.

Perhaps you find yourself tapping your finger to a pattern, or rhythm, that fits around the beat. Rhythm makes the sound of music more interesting.

▼ Some drummers make music from rhythm alone, which can be very exciting and energetic. The shifting patterns of sound have a powerful effect on the listener.

▲ You don't have to be an expert to be a musician! This girl is being shown how to hold a violin and bow properly. A music summer school is a good place to explore the magic of music-making.

Melody and harmony

Try to imagine that a piece of music is a painting. The tune, or **melody**, could be described as the main subject that you focus on. The background sounds, or **harmony**, could be described as the backdrop that gives the scene in the picture its feeling of depth.

A melody is literally a series of musical notes that forms a pattern, which you may recognize and remember – can you sing or hum a nursery rhyme or a football song? Some pieces of music have several different melodies. When a melody appears and reappears in a long piece of music, it often has slight changes or **variations**.

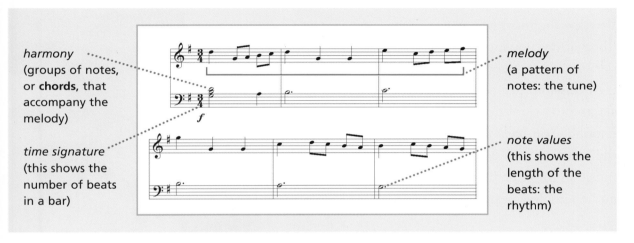

harmony
(groups of notes, or **chords**, that accompany the melody)

time signature
(this shows the number of beats in a bar)

melody
(a pattern of notes: the tune)

note values
(this shows the length of the beats: the rhythm)

▲ Barbershop quartets specialize in unaccompanied "close harmony" singing – the notes in the chords they sing are very close together, and have to be sung accurately.

When two or more notes are played together we call this blend of sounds the harmony. Harmony can influence the mood of the music, such as excitement followed by peacefulness. People who write music follow certain rules of harmony to get the right combination of notes to create a particular effect. It is rather like mixing colours to get different shades when you are painting. Taste in music varies, just like fashions in clothing and pictures. What looks or sounds beautiful to people at one time or in one part of the world may be considered quite ugly by people at another time or in another place.

The invisible musician

When you listen to musicians playing music at a concert, there is one musician you do not see – the composer who has made up the music and written it down. Of course, he or she may have died a long time ago, but it is their music that "flows through" the performer. But there is more to a performance than just playing the notes in the music.

Expression

Perhaps the most important thing about playing, or performing, a piece of music is expression. Just playing or singing the right notes is not enough. You have to convey the emotion that is in the music in order to move the audience's feelings.

Part of a review of Charlotte ▶
Church's CD *Voice of an
Angel* in *Rambles* Magazine

"For me, one of the highlights of the CD is 'Amazing Grace', not for its technical qualities, but rather for its sincere emotional resonance and its lack of artifice. 'Piu Jesu' also has spine-shivering moments, as does 'My Lagan Love' and 'A Lullaby'."

▼ An interview with
the editor of *CDNow*
magazine and a
review of Charlotte's
Enchantment CD

Interviewer: Do you like to perform a song in concert before you record it?

Charlotte: If you read music, it's not that difficult; you just go there and sing it. But to make the most of it and to really get the maximum impact of a song, and to understand it musically, and how it's phrased, and to interpret the words, and everything – you've got to live with it. The longer you live with it, the more comfortable you'll be with it..."

❝Charlotte Church moves with breathtaking ease from classic Broadway . . . to traditional Celtic, film ballads, and even a couple

freedom of expression

of high-operatic numbers . . . What's more, there's a greater freedom of expression and

sense of how to shape a phrase in many of these tracks . . . demonstrating the continued growth of a singularly gifted young artist. ❞

Sarah Chin

Improvisation

Musicians from countries of the West usually play **classical** pieces from printed music. They are expected to follow the printed notes and markings exactly. The music performed at one concert sounds almost identical to the same music performed at another concert.

In jazz, pop and non-Western music, however, there may be very little written music. There is usually just a series of **chords** provided by the players themselves, or taken from a traditional tune that has been handed down. These freer forms of music mainly rely on the musicians making up the music as they go along – we call this **improvisation**. This means that the next time the piece is played it will sound quite different.

People all over the world have always made music. There is a huge tradition of music-making. This book will mainly focus on a tiny part of it – that of the Western world, where music was first collected and written down in the 6th century.

▲ Jazz players such as Branford Marsalis and Herbie Hancock make up the music as they go, improvising on popular tunes.

▲ These musicians are playing Indian music, which involves improvising on a set of notes called a raga. There are more than sixty ragas. Each raga is a type of **scale**, with rules about how and when (what time of day) it should be played.

From monks to madrigals (800–1600)

Western **classical** music developed from the music of the early Christian Church, where medieval monks would chant their prayers. These chants, called plainchant or plainsong, were simple melodies that the monks sang in unison (all together), without harmonies. This type of single-line music is called **monophony**. Many Gregorian chants (named after Pope Gregory I, who lived during the 6th century) are still sung in churches all over the world today.

Part-singing

Gradually, plainsong began to develop. A second group of people would sing a long note, or "drone", on a lower note beneath the **melody**. This second line or part was gradually made more interesting until, by the late 12th century, the music was made up of two or more parts moving independently. This type of music is called **polyphony**.

Notation

In the 11th century, a monk called Guido d'Arezzo invented a new system of musical notation for writing music down. Our modern system of musical notation is based on d'Arezzo's system.

▲ A painting on an illustrated manuscript showing medieval monks singing

▲ Compare this medieval plainsong with today's musical notation (page 5). Both have black shapes (notes) on lines that guide **pitch**.

Medieval minstrels

Monks were not the only musicians in medieval Europe. Minstrels entertained people, in town squares or in rich households, singing songs about love and heroic deeds. Not all minstrels depended on the hand-outs of others, however. Some were important noblemen – even England's King Richard I (the Lionheart) was a notable minstrel.

In medieval times, groups of minstrels would meet to be tested on their ability to compose good poetry and set it to music. In Wales, Celtic minstrels or "bards" called their meetings *eisteddfodau* (sessions). Eisteddfods are still held each year in Wales.

Renaissance music

During the Renaissance period (from roughly 1450 to 1600), music, along with other forms of art, developed quickly, becoming more elaborate. Music also began to spread beyond the Church, as reading and playing music became an important social skill for the wealthier people in society.

▲ The bard and a flower girl singing at the eisteddfod at Bala in Wales

◀ A choir performing in Notre Dame cathedral, France. The English composer Thomas Tallis (c.1505 – 1585) wrote a special work for a large choir. With 40 different parts, all sounding together, it is one of the most complicated and beautiful polyphonic works ever written.

New instruments

The Renaissance was also a time of industrial development. New or updated musical instruments were being made more easily: stringed instruments called viols, keyboard instruments, trumpets, horns and trombones. Many wealthy families played together or with friends as a group, or "consort", of four to six viols, of different sizes and range of **pitch**.

▲ Not long after the Renaissance, many instruments were replaced by newer inventions and were forgotten about. However, in the 20th century, early instruments were rediscovered. Groups like Phantasm, pictured here, now specialize in recreating the original style of playing the music, combining it with a contemporary presentation.

◄ The Sistine Chapel, Rome

see page 18

The Mozart Connection

One of the most popular pieces of Renaissance music today is the *Miserere* by Gregorio Allegri (1582 – 1652). If it weren't for the musical genius of Mozart, however, the work would be unknown today.

Allegri worked for the Pope at St Peter's Cathedral in Rome. The *Miserere* was sung every year in the Sistine Chapel in St Peter's, and the music was "owned" by the chapel – anyone passing it on could be punished. Over a century later, when Allegri's *Miserere* was still being sung at the chapel, it was heard by the composer Wolfgang Mozart. His memory was so good that, after leaving the chapel, he was able to write out the entire work.

Madrigals and meaning

One of the most popular forms of music during the Renaissance was a type of song called the madrigal. It began in Italy but spread throughout Europe in the late 16th century.

A madrigal is usually made up of four or five parts, with one voice to each part. Madrigals use "word-painting" – the notes used for a particular word or phrase in some way reflect its meaning. For example, the word "low" might be sung on a low note, or the word "high" on a high note. Dying, falling, crying, birdsong and even the croak of a frog have been illustrated in madrigal music.

▲ When the printing press was invented in Germany in the 15th century, it became cheaper and easier to produce written copies of music, so many more people became involved in music-making.

▲ An 18th-century painting of a group of madrigal singers

Gesualdo's Jealousy

One Italian composer of madrigals is famous for both his dramatic music and his dramatic life. Carlo Gesualdo (c.1560 – 1613) was an Italian prince. He wrote madrigals with harmonies that were very unusual and advanced for his time. He had a dramatic personality as well – in 1590, he murdered his wife because she had been unfaithful!

Bach and the Baroque (1600–1750)

The period that followed the Renaissance is known as the Baroque, and the Baroque style in music, art and architecture was grand and highly decorated. The Baroque composer most admired today is Johann Sebastian Bach, who was from Germany.

Baroque styles began in Italy. With the introduction of new instruments, including the violin family, composers began to write longer works for larger combinations of instruments. They wrote a line of music for one instrument to play "solo", or alone, with lines for other instruments beneath as **accompaniment**.

Claudio Monteverdi (1567–1643)

Monteverdi was born towards the end of the Renaissance, but his musical outlook was ahead of its time. He was happiest setting music to secular (non-religious) words, and believed that the words, and not the music, were the most important part of the work.

Most of what is known about Monteverdi and his life comes from the many letters he wrote that have survived.

▼ One of the most original Italian Baroque composers was Claudio Monteverdi. In Monteverdi's time, Venice was probably the liveliest city in the world, full of parties, carnivals, theatre and music.

◄ This painting from the Baroque period shows a gathering of people from the new "middle class", being entertained by musicians.

▼ Baroque music reached its peak in the works of J S Bach. Above all, he invented new rules of **harmony**, doing things that other composers never dreamed of, which were often confusing to the listeners of his day.

They show him to be a strong-willed person, determined to "fight his corner" as an over-worked and under-paid court composer. After 12 years working for the Duke of Mantua – and complaining a good deal – Monteverdi achieved his ambition to become musical director at St Mark's Cathedral in Venice.

Monteverdi spent a lot of his time writing madrigals and **operas**. In Monteverdi's time, it was a brand-new form of music, inspired by the Ancient Greeks. Monteverdi did a great deal to develop the form. Although his operas, with their exciting special effects, were extremely popular in Italy, he and his music were soon forgotten after his death. It took 300 years for Monteverdi's music to be rediscovered.

Johann Sebastian Bach
(1685 – 1750)

Johann Sebastian Bach was born in Germany in 1685. His father was a highly respected church organist. Bach's parents both died by the time he was ten. He was then brought up by his elder brother, who was also an organist, and at school he excelled both at music and other studies.

After leaving school, Bach worked first as a court musician, and then became choirmaster, teacher, organist and composer for St Thomas's church in Leipzig, Germany. During his 27 years there, Bach often felt very frustrated with the musical standards: he called one bassoon-player a "nanny-goat bassoonist!"

Bach was a family man, and had a total of 20 children! Some of his children, including his sons Carl Philipp Emanuel and Johann Christian, also became famous composers. Bach's music was studied by composers even after his death in 1750, especially the **Classical** composers.

see pages 16–19

▲ One of the great regrets in Bach's life was that he never met George Handel, whose music he greatly admired. This painting was based on a cartoon of Handel (called "The Charming Brute"), drawn by Handel's "friend" Joseph Goupy.

Patronage

Until the early 18th century, composers were employed by **patrons**. These were rich friends, who paid them to write music. During the 18th century, however, there began to be more public concerts and **operas**, from which composers could earn an income. All the same, until the middle of the 19th century, few composers could manage without the generosity of patrons.

George Handel (1685–1759)

George Handel was born less than a month before Bach, and only 32 km away, in the German town of Halle. The two men both became great organists and Baroque composers. But there were few similarities beyond those.

Although he was a very gifted musician, Bach was not a **child prodigy**. Handel, however, was playing like a talented adult when he was only seven, and was working as a musician by the age of 12. When he was 20, his first opera was staged, and he was soon famous all over Europe. Unlike Bach, who never left Germany, Handel travelled widely. He eventually settled in London, where his music was adored, and he became a wealthy man. When he died in 1759, people all over England grieved.

▲ A Chicago choir and audience in a combined performance of the most popular piece of choral music ever composed – Handel's *Messiah*

Baroque Idols

In Handel's time, spectacular operatic music was written for castrato singers. These were men who had been very gifted singers as boys, and who had an operation so that they kept their high singing voice when they were adults. The castrato sound was unique, as it combined powerful male lungs with a high voice like a female's. Castrato singers had many fans, and so Handel wrote many lead roles in his operas for them.

▲ The life story of the famous castrato Carlo Broschi (1705–1782), known as Farinelli, was made into a film in 1994.

Classical composers (1750–1800)

A huge amount of great music was written in the **Classical** era (1750–1800), even though it was only 50 years long. Between them, Wolfgang Mozart and Joseph Haydn contributed a great deal of that music. Mozart is considered today to be perhaps the greatest musical genius ever. His brain operated like a factory, churning music out, but the products were like precious hand-made goods! Towards the end of the Classical period, Ludwig van Beethoven brought a new power to music that opened the way for the Romantic period that followed.

"Classical" or "classical"
In the world of music, "classical" has two meanings, which can be confusing. Usually, "**classical**" (with a small letter "c") refers to music that is considered serious, and contrasts with popular music.

The other meaning of "Classical" (with a capital "c") refers to the art, architecture and music of Europe in the 18th century, which was inspired by Ancient Greece and Rome.

▲ The Parthenon temple in Athens, Greece, is one of the world's best-preserved classical buildings. Europeans in the 18th century tried to recreate in their art and architecture the elegant simplicity, proportion and symmetry they saw in Ancient Greek and Roman buildings. Composers also tried to reflect these ideals in new musical forms such as the **symphony**.

Joseph Haydn (1732–1809)

Haydn was born in Austria in 1732. His father was a craftsman, and he and his brother lived a simple country life. Haydn was a star choirboy at the Vienna cathedral school, but did not enjoy it. He said he had "more floggings than food"! He left school at the age of 17, with nothing but a few old clothes! For several years, Haydn all but starved. Steadily his reputation grew, and he found work as a music director and composer. Then Haydn's life changed dramatically, when he entered the service of the rich Esterházy family. At their palace in Vienna, he had an orchestra and singers to direct and compose for. His graceful **compositions** perfectly suited the mood of the time, and they soon earned him great fame and wealth. He lived a long life, dying in 1809, when he was 77.

▲ A sample of Haydn's hand-written composition. He once said about his own music: "Since God has given me a cheerful heart, He will forgive me for serving him cheerfully."

▲ Haydn perfected the new musical form of the **symphony**, writing over 100 of them. For this, he is known as the "father of the symphony". He also wrote more than 80 pieces for a new grouping of instruments, the **string quartet**.

Wolfgang Amadeus Mozart
(1756–1791)

Mozart was born in Austria in 1756. By the age of five he was composing good pieces of music. His father, Leopold, was himself a musician, and was determined to make a success of his exceptional son.

Mozart found it difficult to be happy, probably because he felt pressure from his father all his life. Leopold wanted his son to make wise decisions and earn plenty of money. Unfortunately, Mozart found it hard to be grown up, and he managed his financial affairs badly. Unlike Haydn, he could not find a **patron** – he was not willing to change his music to please people. He had to rely on the generosity of wealthy friends and was always in debt. Tragically, he died of typhoid fever when he was only 35, and he died penniless.

▲ Leopold took Wolfgang and his sister Nannerl, who were both child prodigies, on a performing tour of Europe to show off their skills.

◀ Mozart left behind lots of wonderful music that is still very popular today. He is perhaps best-loved today for his **operas**. This is a dramatic scene from a modern version of his opera *Don Giovanni*.

Ludwig van Beethoven
(1770–1827)

Beethoven was born in Bonn, Germany in 1770. His family was poor but musical. His father taught him music, and soon discovered that Ludwig was a **child prodigy**. Beethoven's father pushed him too hard and was very strict, but Beethoven was a natural rebel. Throughout his life he

Beethoven was short, with a large head, protruding teeth and a wild crop of hair. As a person, he was disorganized in everything except what mattered to him most – music.

fought hard against anyone and anything that stood in his way, and was a supporter of the ideas of freedom and equality that caused the Revolution in France. He was determined to fight for his rights as an artist.

Beethoven first became famous as a pianist in Vienna, Austria. The piano was a relatively new instrument at that time, and Mozart and others played it lightly and smoothly. Beethoven imposed his powerful personality, smashing at the keys and sometimes breaking strings! Although Beethoven became a very successful composer, he began to go deaf in his mid-20s. As it got worse he became increasingly bad-tempered. However, he continued composing – hearing the music in his head – until his death in 1827 at the age of 57.

▲ A grand piano made in 1790

Romantic reaction (1800–1900)

During the 19th century, called the Romantic period, composers showed that they believed in artistic freedom and the expression of emotion. They were no longer working for **patrons**, but for the concert-going public. One of the interests of the Romantic audience was the power and beauty of nature, and this was reflected in all the arts of the time.

▲ During the Romantic era, some composers were influenced by the "nationalist" (strongly patriotic) feelings that were growing in Europe, and began to express national identity in their music. For many it involved an attachment to their country, or homeland. One such composer was Edvard Grieg (1843–1907), from Norway, who is buried beside a fjord like the one pictured here, close to his home.

▼ A portrait of Schubert, sometimes called the "poet of music"

Franz Schubert (1797–1828)

One of the great early Romantic composers was the Austrian, Franz Schubert. Much of his music is rooted in the **Classical** style, but he also perfected a new Romantic form of song (called *Lieder* in German), and wrote more than 600 of them. Schubert died aged 31, but in his relatively short life he composed at a great speed (almost as fast as Mozart!) and so has left lots of music for us to enjoy.

Virtuoso Cult

A virtuoso is a musician who plays to a standard that is brilliant and awe-inspiring, and in the Romantic period virtuoso musicians were huge stars. Some virtuosos were even thought to have **supernatural powers**. The tall, dark, Italian violinist Nicolò Paganini (1782–1840) was a fantastic showman, employing tricks such as "accidentally" breaking a string on his violin, in order to show that he could still play brilliantly on just three strings.

▲ The great Hungarian composer Franz Liszt (1811–1886) was also a piano virtuoso. This cartoon shows the kind of impression his playing could make!

Richard Wagner (1813–1883)

The German composer Richard Wagner took Romantic ideals to their extreme, writing music of great emotional force that included new, strange-sounding harmonies. He created a new style of **opera** he called "music-drama". These very dramatic works used bigger orchestras, which could play very loudly. Wagner wrote the words and music as well as planning the scenery and costume. He wanted complete control over his productions. Eventually he built his own opera house in Bayreuth, Germany.

◄ A scene from Wagner's opera *The Flying Dutchman*. The writer Oscar Wilde once poked fun at Wagner's music, saying: "I like Wagner's music better than anybody's. It is so loud that one can talk the whole time without other people hearing what one says."

Modern musicians (1900–2002)

▲ The French composer Claude Debussy (1862–1918) was one of the first modern composers. He was inspired by new sights and sounds, such as the orchestral music of Indonesia, known as gamelan.

Today, you can hear musicians performing every kind of historic music, from Gregorian chant to Wagnerian **opera**, as well as **classical** and popular styles that have developed in the last hundred years! Since the beginning of the 20th century, there has been more experimentation than ever before: the development of new instruments that use modern electronic technology, and the growth of many new forms of popular music, including musicals, jazz, rock and the fast-moving world of pop.

Classical music

Around the beginning of the 20th century, many European composers began to break away from Romantic styles of music. The Romantic style did not end abruptly one day, with "modern" classical styles beginning the next. In fact, in the 20th century it is not always possible to call something "classical" or "popular", as so many pieces of music lie somewhere in between.

Experimental music

During the 1920s, composers began experimenting with the forms and structures of music. In the late 1930s, the US composer John Cage (1912–1992) started to write music that would be different each time it was played. Some of his early pieces require a "prepared piano" – a piano with objects (such as screws and rubber bands) placed under the strings to make its sounds unpredictable.

In the 1960s Karlheinz Stockhausen (born 1928) was one of the first to produce electronic music using synthesizers. These instruments have given music a new quality – they produce an electric sound signal that is carried by cable to an amplifier and loudspeaker. They are widely used by both pop musicians and modern composers.

▲ The Royal Ballet performing Igor Stravinsky's *The Rite of Spring* in 1987. In 1913, at the first performance of this ballet, a riot broke out. The audience was outraged by the story of a girl dancing herself to death, and by Stravinsky's music, which was unlike anything that had been heard before.

Minimal, or process music, emerged in the 1950s, and is made up of short phrases that are repeated over and over again, changing very slightly each time. Some people think it is a boring sound that is popular because it is easy to listen to; others say it is pure and relaxing.

◄ The opera *Akhnaten* (1983), set in Ancient Egypt, was written by the minimalist composer Philip Glass (born 1937).

Musicals

Musicals are plays that combine acting, singing and dancing. They developed out of the 19th-century tradition of light **opera** (or operetta) that was made popular in England by Gilbert and Sullivan. William Gilbert (1836–1911) wrote funny, rhyming words and Arthur Sullivan (1842–1900) set them to pleasant, uncomplicated music. They often poked fun at the fashions of the day.

▲ In 2000, the story of the Gilbert and Sullivan partnership was made into a film called *Topsy Turvy*, which featured their operetta *The Mikado*.

▲ One of the most famous composers of musicals today is Andrew Lloyd Webber (born 1948). His show *Cats* is the longest-running musical in the history of the theatre.

In the 20th century, musicals became as popular in the USA as they were in Europe. By the 1930s and 40s, the most famous composers in the world of stage and film musicals were American. Some of the most popular musicals were written by Richard Rodgers (1902–1979), who wrote the music, and Oscar Hammerstein II (1895–1960), who wrote the words. These include *Oklahoma!*, *Carousel*, and *The King and I*.

George Gershwin (1898–1937) and Leonard Bernstein (1918–1990) also bridged the gap between **classical** and popular music by bringing the American sounds of jazz and Latin-American dance rhythms into their music.

Jazz

Jazz is a broad term covering many different styles that have developed since the early days of Dixieland jazz in New Orleans, Louisiana, in the southern USA.

Jazz has its roots in the days of slavery. During the 18th and 19th centuries, when Africans were taken to the Americas as slaves, most were made to work on plantations in America's southern states. It was back-breaking work and they were treated with cruelty, but many of the slaves soothed themselves with work-songs that used familiar African rhythms. As Christianity spread amongst the slaves' communities, African-Americans also developed their own religious music – spirituals and gospel music.

After the Civil War in America ended in 1865 and slavery was abolished, African-Americans had to struggle to survive. They had freedom but not equality with white Americans. In the poor areas in the South, people told the story of their hardship in a song style known as the "blues".

The first New Orleans bands were brass bands – six or seven musicians playing cornets, trombones and tubas. Many of these instruments had been left behind after the American Civil War by the military brass bands of the defeated Southern army. ▶

▼ A 19th-century painting showing slaves working in the cotton fields

Dixieland sound

By the end of the 19th century, jazz had made its home in New Orleans. In this traditional style of jazz, the players jumble up the notes in their own way, and the soloists all play their **melodies** at the same time, cleverly mixing them together. In the 1920s the style became known as Dixieland.

▲ By 1930, the centre of the jazz world had shifted from the South to the North of the USA. The Cotton Club, in New York's Harlem district, gave black musicians the chance of becoming stars, but only white people were allowed into the audience.

Louis ("Satchmo") Armstrong (1901–1971)

Louis Armstrong is one of the most famous names in jazz history. He was born in New Orleans into a poor family. When he was 11 he fired a gun in the street as a joke and as a result he was sent to a reform school for boys who had broken the law. At the school he learnt to play the cornet, which is an instrument a little like a trumpet.

After leaving the school, he began his career as a jazz musician, and soon became famous for his gravelly singing voice and for his solo trumpet-playing. From the 1930s he also appeared in several films.

▼ Louis Armstrong in 1968. His nickname "Satchmo" (short for "satchel mouth") refers to the shape of his mouth.

Billie Holiday (1915–1959)

Eleanora Harris was born in 1915. She took the name Billie Holiday as a stage name, and was singing in the jazz clubs of Harlem by the time she was 15. She was a troubled person and turned to alcohol and drugs, which led to her early death in 1959.

In her songs, she expressed great emotion. Her voice was husky (some compare it to a saxophone), and she kept her style plain so the words were always clear.

Billie Holiday's songs often dealt with difficult subjects, such as the racism that existed in America's Deep South. ▶

Saxophone

The saxophone, a brass instrument, is named after Adolphe Sax, who invented it in 1846. By the 1930s it had become one of the main instruments in jazz. Sax made the instrument in fourteen sizes, but only four are common today: soprano, alto, tenor and baritone.

◀ The great saxophonist Joshua Redman. He plays the tenor sax.

White jazz

The growing popularity of jazz-style dance music in the 1930s attracted many white musicians. Band leaders sweetened the jazz sound, even adding orchestral instruments, and developed the style known as "swing". Later, in the 1950s, white artists took another jazz form, called "boogie", and transformed it into a new style of popular music – rock 'n' roll.

Elvis Presley (1935–1977)

Elvis Presley was probably the greatest of the rock 'n' roll stars. He was good-looking, had a rich singing voice, and a style of dancing that shocked many people. He merged the blues and gospel sounds of his black musician friends with the white tradition of "country" music. Elvis became a national star only a few years after recording his first song. The first of his 94-million-selling **singles** was *Heartbreak Hotel* (1956). After serving in the army he also became a film star and continued his singing career. He died of heart-failure when he was only 42.

Elvis Presley, the "King of Rock 'n' Roll", ▶ singing *Jailhouse Rock*

The Beatles

In the 1960s, pop music was born. Teenagers had more money to spend on singles recorded by their favourite groups. The entertainment industry knew how to catch their interest. Of course, bands that had talent, looks and character were the easiest to sell, and the Beatles had all these ingredients and more. Many people were shocked by the effect the band had on the screaming teenagers at their concerts.

Goodbye, Britain—Hello New York

Daily Mirror

Fans on a roof at London Airport wave goodbye to the Beatles yesterday.

3d. Saturday, February 8, 1964   No. 18,704

YEAH! YEAH! U.S.A!

That old Beatlemania hits New York . . . a screaming girl tries to get nearer the Beatles.

Paul, Ringo, George and John answer questions at the Press conference.

FATHER FLIES TO GET IRENE

PRINCESS Irene of Holland, whose romance has started a constitutional crisis, is going home today.

'Engagement news soon'

From BARRIE HARDING
New York, Friday

5,000 scream 'welcome' to the Beatles

FIVE thousand screaming, chanting teenagers—most of them playing truant from school—gave the Beatles a fantastic welcome here today.

△ Since the 1990s, photographs of pop groups have appeared on a vast range of products. Product manufacturers discovered that pop stars helped sell their products, and music executives saw that the products would draw attention to their stars, and earn them more money.

Rock music

In the 1970s and 80s, groups like the Rolling Stones and Led Zeppelin introduced heavier, more aggressive styles of music called hard rock and heavy metal. Punk rock was even more angry. In its **lyrics** and fashions, it aimed to break society's rules of decency and civilized behaviour.

Dance music

Pop music mostly has a fast beat, a lively tune and happy words – designed to get the listener dancing. In the 1970s, 80s and 90s there have been lots of different kinds of dance music, such as soul, disco, hip-hop and techno. Pop stars such as Madonna and the Spice Girls also reached a new level of success, becoming famous all over the world.

World Music

At the end of the 20th century, pop music, which originated in the USA and has been dominated by the West ever since, opened up to include musical traditions from other parts of the world. These performers play music that is native to their country, sometimes combined with ideas from Western pop music, such as Western harmonies.

△ Ladysmith Black Mambazo performing at London's biggest concert hall, The Royal Albert Hall

Time line

Developments in European music

Music is made by minstrels and monks

Guido d'Arezzo invents new system of musical notation

Polyphony develops in church music

Musical composition becomes more complex

Madrigal composition develops in Italy

New musical instruments
Printed music begins to appear
Music-making becomes more popular

Madrigals popular all over Europe
Violin family is introduced

Claudio Monteverdi develops opera in Italy

Century of great composers (Bach, Handel, Haydn, Mozart, Beethoven) and new musical forms (symphony, string quartet).
Concert-going public develops.
Music and other art forms become more emotionally dramatic (especially Wagner's new "music-dramas")

Era of experimentation in music
New styles include musicals, jazz, rock and pop

1000
1100
1200
1300
1400
1500
1600
1700
1800
1900
2000

Major historical events in Europe

Norman conquest of England (1066)

Richard I (the Lionheart) becomes King of England (1198)

King John signs Magna Carta (1215), limiting royal power

Black Death kills over one third of Europe's population

Printing press invented in Germany

Spanish Armada defeated by English (1588)

Scientific revolution in Europe begins

French Revolution (1789–99)

From 1830, revolutionary movements in France, Germany, Poland, Italy

First World War (1914–18)
Second World War (1939–45)
Communist regimes topple (1988–92)

Glossary

accompaniment Music that is played to support the sound of the main instrument or voice part.

child prodigy A child who has exceptional ability.

chord Two or more notes played together.

classical (with a small "c") Refers to music of the past that is considered "serious", more or less follows established rules and has "stood the test of time". It contrasts with "popular" music, which is considered less complex, "light" and only relevant to the era in which it is written.

Classical (with a capital "c") Refers to European music from the 18th century.

composition A piece of music that has been written down.

harmony A system of chords in music. The rules of harmony are different in different parts of the world, and they have changed over time.

improvisation Making up music as you go along, usually within boundaries set by the musical style.

lyrics The words of a song.

melody A series of musical notes that forms a pattern, which you may recognize and remember.

monophony A piece of music where everybody sings or plays the same melody all together, with no accompaniment.

opera A kind of play set to music, where all the words are sung instead of spoken.

patrons The term used for employers of Renaissance and Baroque composers – for example the Church, royalty or members of the nobility.

pitch How high or low a note is.

polyphony Music that consists of several tunes which move independently but weave together to create a harmonious sound.

scale A fixed series of notes, moving from lowest to highest and back again. Most pieces of music are based on scales.

single A recording of one hit song.

string quartet A group made up of two violins, a viola and a cello. Also the name of a piece of music written for that group of instruments.

supernatural powers An ability to see and do things that are usually thought to be impossible.

symphony A composition, usually for orchestra, that consists of a set of "movements" or sections (normally four).

variations A form of music in which a familiar melody is changed or rearranged.

Index